Brandly Speaking

by Tom Sitati

Edited by Caroline Kimutai,
Editor, MANAGEMENT Magazine

Illustrated by Patrick Gathara,
Cartoonist, Nation Media Group

Published by Brandscape Africa Foundation
www.brandscapeafrica.org

ISBN 978-9966-7322-5-5

Dedication

To my parents

Branding is not a choice; it is a lifestyle!

If I could summarise this book into one sentence, it would be: Branding is definitely not a choice; it is a lifestyle. You either (intentionally) brand yourself, product, service, organisation etc or, someone else will do the branding for you. I can bet that 8 out 10 times when you allow someone else to brand you, you won't like what you hear or see. That is how core the brand is to our lives and the reason why more and more people are investing billions of dollars in building their brands. It is worth the investment because despite a gloomy economy, consumers are willing to pay a premium for a brand even if it means spending money they don't have.

Months before the 2010 World Cup was held for the first time on the African continent, leading soft drink maker Coca-Cola sponsored a glamorous tour of the World Cup trophy across 52 countries around the world. The Coca-Cola brand was literally living on the fun side of life as its officials globe trotted on a branded jet show-casing the pure gold trophy that only presidents and players of teams that have won the football tournament are allowed to touch. You don't need to be a brand expert to conclude that 2010 was a 'Coke year' in Africa.

Indeed, branding is not a choice. Everyone from presidents, charities, journalists, preachers and even the beggars on the busy highways are branding themselves. Unfortunately, this book does not delve into the nuts and bolts of branding and neither is it a quick fix 'How to' prescription book. Tom Sitati has put together a collection of his thoughts inform of articles that were published in the *Business Daily* - a Kenyan business newspaper, websites and presentations he has delivered at various local and international forums.

The articles are short, interesting and full of practical examples of the things you see around and interact with. He presents his thoughts in a refreshing perspective and demystifies what we thought was rocket science. Sitati's observations are backed by facts, research and reports from globally respected scholars and authors.

This book takes you on an exciting 'brand journey' across various continents from Africa, Asia to Europe where we see the interesting links between nations and their product brands. Kenya, like many African nations, is painfully learning that good governance determines the success of a nation brand. From Europe, Sitati shares an inspiring story from Germany and how it rose from a shameful past to become home to many of the world's top brands. He also takes a candid look at the Asian tiger, its popular 'Made in China' brand and the various challenges it is facing.

For those in business, beware! There is a new virus in town – brand myopia syndrome. Sitati challenges entrepreneurs and those in management to step out of the proverbial box and expand their horizons. Even if you are not in the business of making profit, you cannot avoid branding. If you have a strong brand, it will be much easier to attract funding and community support.

There are very few books that talk about brands in Africa or from an African perspective - this is one book that will add to the body of knowledge.

Caroline Kimutai, April 2012

Are you suffering from brand myopia?

What separates great brands from the good and ordinary ones? The gospel according to Prof Ted Levitt.

How can a brand ensure its continued growth? Forty-eight years ago, *Harvard Business Review* (HBR) published an article by Theodore Levitt, a little known lecturer in business administration. The article, titled *Marketing Myopia*, is to date one of the most popular the HBR has ever published and remains a valuable reference for brands wishing to ensure long-term growth. The article won the McKinsey Award in 1960. Prof Levitt is, of course, more famous for coining the term "globalisation" and, upon his death in 2006, Harvard marketing

Prof Stephen A. Greyser eulogised him thus: "If you had an all-star team of management thinkers ... Ted Levitt would be the [marketing] guy from Harvard Business School."

As I read through the article for the umpteenth time, it got me thinking; have Kenyan brands learnt from the article? Are the lessons still relevant almost five decades later? According to an article in *Business Week* published upon Prof Levitt's death, "...nothing made him happier than when top executives— 'important people in important companies,' in his phrase — took those ideas and ran with them." I wonder which brands Prof Levitt may be smiling down upon from the afterlife.

What business are you really in?

According to Prof Levitt, sustained growth depends on two things. First, how broadly one defines the business and, second, how carefully one gauges customers' needs. Industries and, by implication, brands are guilty of defining themselves too narrowly and this stifles their long-term growth. Prof Levitt used the example of the railroad industry which stagnated after years of appearing virtually indispensable. According to the article, the industry did not stop growing because customers required less passenger or freight transportation. It didn't decline because of the advent of cars, trucks, planes or even telephones. It declined because management defined the business too narrowly. Management failed to see that railroads were really in the transportation business and not the railroad business. They had defined the business from their "product" perspective rather than from the customers' perspective. The East African governments persist in the myopia Prof Levitt described before our independence. It is no wonder that Rift Valley Railways, a relic from the colonial days, is a tough nut to crack.

Today, many brands continue to define themselves too narrowly. This can be seen especially in the Information and Communication Technology (ICT) industry. The industry still has brands thinking they are in the "computer industry". Others that provide "internet services" still define themselves as internet companies. They do so even as telecoms have grown to be the largest supplier of internet connectivity through the mobile phone. They fail to realise what the customer really wants and define themselves by the mere "tool" applied to satisfy the customers' needs. Commodities such as tea, cocoa, coffee and precious stones, which developing countries dominate, are already redefined beyond the mere product. Unfortunately, the producers, who are now busy singing the recently coined "value addition" mantra, had their heads bowed and brows sweating in the toils of production when the branding ship sailed by.

No such thing as a growth industry

When Prof Levitt declared that "In truth, there is no such thing as a growth industry", many heads turned. What they had not read, or chose not to take notice of, was his next sentence which reads: "There are only companies organised and operated to create and capitalise on growth opportunities." This is essentially an issue of brand positioning. Brands will not thrive and grow for the long term because of riding the wave of an industry. Examples of hitherto "growth industries" abound. The dry cleaning industry had its era, the grocery store had its time, and electrical utilities rose only to plateau and eventually decline. These are just some of the examples cited in *Marketing Myopia*. The most recent big burst of the growth industry bubble was the Dot Coms, which had a much shorter bask in the limelight of the growth industry myth. Closer home, the mobile telephony industry and its brands, which appeared a sure bet, are not what they seem to be. Time will tell that positioning a brand based on this narrow thinking is a sure road to brand perdition that promises no redemption.

Almost half a century on, marketing myopia among our brands persists. It is what is separating the great brands from the good and ordinary ones. Many brands still define themselves by narrow categories that become extinct as consumer needs change. The competitive environment in every industry is such that only the great will survive for the long term while the good and ordinary can begin writing their eulogies. Those that learn from the lessons of the Prof Levitt's evergreen article will successfully deliver themselves from the claws of brand myopia and find themselves in the comfortable arms of brand success.

© Tom Sitati, 26th March 2012

Nothing micro about brand building

Every microfinance institution should endeavour to build its brand to a level where people would pay to associate with it.

In the world of brands, there is a select few brands that occupy a sacred place in our hearts and minds. We seem to cherish these brands so much that we are even willing to pay to be associated with them. For some reason, sane and sober human beings will fight should anybody try and disparage the brands they cherish. These brands come from all sorts of sectors – automotive, sports, non-profits, education, household and many others. What they have in common is that they seem to transcend the barriers created by continents, nations, industries or sectors. They seem not to belong to the simple boxes we human beings conveniently place around phenomenon so as to understand and relate to them easily.

What is it that great brands possess that the others do not? They all ultimately appeal to our emotions. It is for this reason that the terms "micro" and "finance" in microfinance institutions (MFIs) may find themselves redundant if we are to build truly great brands that will achieve the visions MFIs set out to achieve when they were founded.

Many organisations in the microfinance sector now find themselves undergoing "transformation". These changes are bound to impact on their brands. The purpose of our discussion is to unearth the brand challenges faced by transforming microfinance institutions and ultimately tackle how best to deal with them. To do this we first need to understand what brand is all about.

What does brand really mean and does it have relevance in the microfinance sector? Transformation has various connotations and we will need to agree on the context in which we view it. What does transformation really entail? What does it aim to achieve? Microfinance brands have some unique characteristics that differentiate them from other organisations. We will need to highlight these unique characteristics so as to understand what challenges these brands face as they undergo transformation. This will in turn assist us in understanding how best to overcome the brand challenges that come with transformation. This discussion addresses the microfinance sector in general, tackling it as one brand though acknowledging the fact that the sector does have unique, differentiated brands.

What is a great brand?

On deep analysis, life can be simplified in one word – relationships. We maintain relationships with those we feel are able to come through for us as we do the same in return. Promise making and keeping is at the heart of relationships. Brands, having grown to become an integral part of our lives, find themselves following the patterns of our lives. The brands we have come to admire, cherish and even fight for, despite

sometimes overwhelming evidence to the contrary, are those
that we best relate to. They are the brands that have somehow
been able to relate to what we relate to. They are the brands that
have been able to tug at our emotional cords and appeal to our
hearts. These are the brands that stand for something we believe
in. These are the brands that make promises to us and
consistently keep them. That is why we say that a brand is a
promise and *a great brand is a promise made and a promise
kept*. A great brand will be the guiding star for the entire
organisation, not just the communication, business development
or marketing departments.

Is brand relevant to MFIs?

Branding has long been considered a preserve of the
commercial, profit-driven sector. It is only recently that brand
has gained prominence in the non-profit sector. More
organisations in the microfinance sector now realise that brand
building is not really a choice. To paraphrase the unwritten law
of branding, when no intentional efforts are applied to build and
manage a brand, then the sum of all rumours, anecdotes,
impressions, myths, become the brand. The choice players in the
microfinance industry have is whether to manage their brand
intentionally so as to achieve their visions or to gamble with
them with possibly detrimental consequences.

Players in the microfinance industry need to intentionally create
and manage their brands. They need to find what they stand for,
what unique promise they make in a competitive market and
how to keep it as an entire organisation. It is crucial that
everybody in the organisation knows, understands and lives the
brand promise because we know not the hour when the brand
may need to rise to the occasion and prove that it, indeed, keeps
its promise and deserves be considered a truly great brand. It
would be a pity if, after brilliant promises have been made, the
customers, donors, communities and partners find the brand
unable or unwilling to keep them. It would almost be better no
such grand promise was made in the first place.

MFI brands must be intentionally managed to appeal to customers, communities they work with, donors that support them, governments that facilitate their existence and regulate them. Well managed brands also attract and keep the best employees. A great brand is the result of going the whole hog by making sure the brand is intentionally defined, meticulously managed, clearly communicated and ultimately lived by all staff.

The 'What' and 'Why' of MFI transformation

MFIs began with a social mission, many of them having their origins in the donor supported non-governmental sector. Their role at inception was to enable those mostly in the 'Third World' who were unable to access financial services to do so in order to raise their standards of life. Microfinance was basically an intervention aimed at addressing the issue of poverty in society. Many of the organisations remained relatively unstructured yet extremely successful, so successful that some even began competing with mainstream financial institutions such as banks. In countries like the Philippines, Nigeria and Uganda, for example, the last decade has seen a drive towards a formal structuring of these microfinance institutions. Transformation has come through government regulation in the mentioned examples but transformation is not necessarily about government regulation. It is about restructuring the institutions in a number of ways so as to increase efficiency and accountability. These include the standardisation of systems, procedures, governance structures, risk management and, where there is legislation, reporting and surveillance by the central banks. These activities, which have been alien to many microfinance institutions, have come with challenges but seem to be the inevitable trend globally.

Some of the reasons why transformation is inevitable include the fact that credit from microfinance institutions is more expensive than credit from commercial banks. It is also no secret that MFIs have limited financial resources, a factor that limits the achievement of their social goals. Transformation in some cases allows MFIs access to more and cheaper funds.

Another factor is that many of the institutions are not up to scratch in areas such as organisational structure, personnel, systems, procedures and governance, with several having no oversight on their activities despite commanding huge numbers of clients. This need for oversight, specifically from central banks becomes a critical issue now that in some countries, transformation comes with the licence to mobilise deposits from clients. Some transformation regimes such as the one in Uganda are geared towards creating deposit-taking microfinance institutions. This radical shift demands several fundamental changes of MFIs.

The MFI brand and the transformation challenge

What is the essence of microfinance institutions? What makes them unique, credible and differentiated from customers' perspective (the only one that really matters)? What promise do they make as brands? What challenges will they face as they seek to transform?

1. MFI brands are open and friendly, not viewing those they work with as typical "customers" but partners or "members". Will the shift to seeing their partners as customers from whom they must "milk" the most money result in an alienation that may affect the numbers negatively?
2. MFI brands have maintained relatively informal and flexible structures. Will the rigid structures demanded as they transform work to the detriment of MFIs? Will the benefits that the informality MFIs have grown accustomed to diminish their effectiveness?
3. MFI brands, because of their social purpose, have generally attracted people who feel passionate about the organisation's goals. Will the new personnel they hire at board, management and operational levels feel as passionate about the brands' noble mission? Will this affect the impact the MFIs have on communities?
4. MFI brands have an autonomy that has allowed them to relate to clients in a manner that allows them to make

quick decisions, go out of their way, and even sometimes break procedure to meet their clients' needs. Will the sometimes stringent conditions that come with regulation and "big brother" Central Bank watching dilute this essence that made MFIs a delight to work with? Will the boards, management and staff have the capacity to work under the new conditions and still deliver on their brand promise to communities they work with?

5. MFI brands are close to their clients, building even personal relationships that go beyond financial transactions. Will the bankers who will inevitably come on board to satisfy the key human resource gaps that must be filled for successful transformation, and who are used to "doing a job" rather than "championing a cause," understand and assimilate this new paradigm? Will they be willing or able to change orientation so as to keep the MFI brand aligned to its original mission and vision?

6. MFI brands have usually approached issues from the point of looking to solve the clients' problem first. The profit motive sometimes makes organisations lose the obvious fact that brands only grow when they are able to relate to the customer. Will MFIs find themselves blinded by profit and lose the customer's heart in the process?

7. MFI brands are not always about finance and originally did not really play in the financial but more in the social sector. Their goal is to solve society's social problems. Will transformation where MFIs now seem firmly thrust in the financial sector not create a status issue, with MFIs being viewed as inferior to banks and unregulated MFIs being seen as inferior to the regulated MFIs? Will this not have an impact on both the communities MFIs work with and the staff?

8. MFI brands are known for giving credit, not mobilising savings. How easy will it be for customers to shift their viewpoint? Will customers be able to relate to MFIs as the new reservoirs for their savings?

9. MFI brands have been valued, not for their ability to realise profits, but their ability to impact society positively. Will regulation by central banks, whose bias is prudent financial management, result in mission drift for

MFIs? Will MFIs please the regulator or focus on their social mission of restoring self worth and dignity to the impoverished?

10. MFI brands have been known for their extensive reach, even to geographical areas no financial institution would venture because it sometimes did not make short-term financial sense. Will the short-term need to watch the bottom line result in capitalistic tendencies that have hitherto not been the outlook of MFIs?

Meet the challenges

First, MFIs must clearly define their brand strategies. They must be crystal clear about what their visions and missions are as well as what they stand for as brands. This should be the guiding light as they undergo transformation and any other activity for that matter.

Second, MFIs must be clear about why they are transforming. They must not lose the way because of the need to conform to regulation. Doing this would be tantamount to making the process of transformation equivalent to digging one's own grave, where the eventual certificate obtained will be the equivalent of a death certificate.

Third, and arguably most important, MFI brands must remember that, eventually, branding is really about relationships. As they transform, MFI brands should ensure they build the right capacity as led by their brand strategies. Being in service, people are a crucial part of the delivery of their brand promises. MFI brands should consider they only recruit and retain those that have bought into their brand. For those already on board, the brand must be internalised continuously to ensure the brand promise is known, understood and ultimately lived by all, right from board level to the field level staff.

When it comes to brand building there is nothing micro about it. Every MFI should endeavour to build its brand to a level where people would pay to associate with it.

This was a presentation given at the School of Applied Microfinance, Mombasa, Kenya on 10th September 2009.

The Herculean TASK

Ask not what your profession can do for you—ask what you can do for your profession.

When I first heard of the actuarial profession, what stood out was not the complexity of what the professionals do, but the scarcity of practising actuaries. I was also taken aback by the ability of such a crucial profession to remain a big secret of the insurance industry. As I researched, I realised that the actuarial profession plays a critical role and equated its current positioning to the Biblical illustration of a candle placed under the table.

It is encouraging that the theme of the Actuarial Society's annual convention this year is focused on putting this candle on

the table. It is also encouraging that the profession is now
thinking seriously of raising that proverbial candle towards the
ceiling to provide the guiding light for crucial business decisions
across industries. The 2009 theme "Branding the actuarial
profession" is most appropriate.

Looking through what is documented as The Actuarial Society of
Kenya's (TASK) role, one point is particularly illustrative of the
way forward. It, incidentally, happens to be the final point: "To
broaden the scope of the profession". Strategic branding is the
perfect tool to help take the actuarial profession forward.

To kick off the discussion, let us briefly talk about your role as
professionals in building the actuarial profession brand. It is the
little known mystical Lebanese American artist, poet, and writer
Khalil Gibran and not John F Kennedy, as is widely assumed,
who in his 1925 works titled *New Frontier* wrote: "Ask not what
your country can do for you—ask what you can do for your
country." J F Kennedy's appropriation of the timeless phrase is
a direct result of his greater personal brand. It is this power of
branding that I wish to invite each one of you to tap into and
build your profession. You may wish to take a moment and ask
yourself: what can I, as an actuarial professional, talk about with
more authority than anybody else? As you think, remember: ask
not how TASK shall build your profession, but what you can do
to build the actuarial profession.

What is branding?

There are so many definitions of branding and, as the concept
takes on more importance in every sphere of life, the definitions
seem to keep multiplying. For purposes of our discussion, let us
look at branding as *the process of intentionally creating one's
own undisputed space in the mind of relevant publics*.

The concept of "space in the mind" exploits the nature of human
beings to appropriate names, attributes and meaning to

whatever phenomena they encounter. When we meet a new person and do not know their name, we may give them a name of our choice, pick out a distinguishing feature, be it behavioural or physical, and brand them thus. We do the same with products, services, companies, countries and even professions. How we appropriate space in our minds and therefore brand various phenomena may range from functional attributes, through to functional benefits, emotional benefits and, eventually, aspirational benefits. The greatest brands appeal to our aspirations.

Where does the actuarial profession find itself on this ladder? Is it able to rise above its technical, mathematical origins? Is it able to free itself from the box that is the insurance and pensions industry and venture into the deeper and wider ocean of opportunity? Does it appeal to the aspirations of industry leaders and future potential professionals who are still groping in the dark?

What is a profession?

A profession possesses three features that distinguish it from any other craft carried out to pass time and make ends meet. First, it must be based on specialised knowledge and training. Second, it must have a shared code of ethics and third, it must be perceived to render objective counsel.

What causes some professions to be perceived as superior to others? It is probably the fact that they are both *relevant to most of the population and that they have consistently occupied a single space in the mind of that population over time?* Is the actuarial profession relevant to a sizeable proportion of the population? At this stage, is it even well known and understood? Has the actuarial profession shown this relevance to a majority of the population? Has the actuarial profession been able to occupy a single space in the mind of the population? Are you making an intentional effort to build the actuarial profession's brand?

My understanding of the actuarial profession is that it is able to
"make financial sense of the future". If there is anything the
world needs, especially in the "return to sensibility economy"
era we are in, it is certainty. Measurement and management of
risk is no longer a luxury. The gambling days are gone forever.

Actuary's core competencies such as "financial architecture" or
"social mathematics", to borrow some colloquial terms, really
need to be looked at as hygiene factors in the drive to brand the
profession. Even at a personal level, the core skills of an actuary
need to be taken as a given, as each professional seeks to
position the profession at a higher level. In this way, actuary
shall stand out as the great profession that it is. Remember that
the greatest brands operate at an aspiration rather than a
technical level. What are the aspirations that you can latch on to
as a professional so as to appropriately position the actuarial
brand? How do you, both at a personal and collective level find a
way to play the wider role you deserve to play at a national,
regional and even international level?

Creating space for the actuarial profession

The process of building a brand takes time and must be both
intentional and disciplined. Below are a few tips on the way
forward as you continue the journey towards building the
actuarial brand:

1. Know what your profession stands for – what is your
    unique promise of value?
2. Know your target audience – who do you wish to address?
3. Know your competitors – who else is running a similar
    race?
4. Define your brand promise – document your brand
    promise: it must be a singular way in which you wish to be
    perceived from a wider perspective and should be
    anchored in real competence. What do you want your
    profession to be the default for?

5. Communicate and live your brand – ensure your brand is communicated and experienced at every touch point. In the actuarial industry, the ball falls squarely with each actuarial professional.

Building an actuarial profession brand

Because brands are by their very nature unique, no single formula can be applied to building brands. The tips outlined below can be tailored and applied to building the actuarial professional brand:

1. Build a large and relevant network. Remember that while most of us were asleep, the world moved online.
2. Increase your virtual and physical visibility.
3. Constant communication to the right audience is critical.
4. Take leadership roles in crosscutting initiatives.
5. And if the right initiatives do not exist, create your own.

Actuary has the potential to build its brand beyond technical competence used only in the insurance and pensions industries. It is upon each practitioner to take up the mantle of proving, day after day, what the actuarial profession stands for. I do not have the answers but hope the questions posed here have planted the seed that can germinate and grow the actuarial profession.

I leave you to ponder, but not for too long. It is not intentions but deliberate, consistent and focused actions over the long term by each actuarial professional that will build a great of the profession.

This is a presentation made on 17th July 2009 at The Actuarial Convention 2009 hosted by The Actuarial Society of Kenya (TASK) at Laico Regency Hotel, Nairobi, Kenya.

Era of 'big small brands'

Ladies and gentlemen, here is introducing brands that offer unlimited "long tail" variety of small (and big) brands to the consumer in one place.

The publication of Naomi Klein's anti-branding treatise entitled "No Logo" in 2001 got many brand enthusiasts thinking about the future of brands and branding. Was the "almighty brand" on its deathbed? Was the very existence of brands threatened by a heightened global sense of social justice and mass protests against their seemingly unbridled power?

Chris Anderson's 2006 publication, *The Long Tail*, is probably the best pointer to where brands are headed. While the author does not directly tackle the issue of brands, he discusses how unlimited choice is creating virtually unlimited demand. His book's slant indicates that we are in for a major tectonic shift. One could argue that is already happening right before our eyes.

Brands are essentially the beacons we use to navigate today's ever complicated world. Through research in the music industry, author Chris Anderson came up with proof that there is more business to be made out of the "non-hits" category put together than there is to be made of the hits. When interviewed, Ecast CEO Robbie Vann-Adibe was unable to guess the correct percentage of the more than 10,000 albums his company sold, had managed to sell at least one track per quarter. The right figure is an astonishing 98 per cent!

Because of new distribution systems such as the internet and lower overheads, retailers were not constrained to only selling hits. Most of the market was actually in the "non-hits" category. The long tail phenomenon means we now have unlimited access to a hitherto inaccessible myriad of small brands from virtually anywhere in the world. Put together, these small brands from around the world can actually outsell the relatively few huge brands.

Levelled playing field

Thomas Friedman's *The World is Flat,* is another book that sheds some light on the future of brands and branding. The basic take of Friedman's book is "how globalisation—taken up to an almost sky-scraping height and down to an even more unimaginable depth—has levelled the 'playing field' and made possible ...the 'virtual' compression of geographic space and time..."

The levelled playing field of the flat world means brands now face more competition and more opportunity, some of it from very unlikely sources. If five years ago you whispered in the ear of any internet service provider CEO that they would be looking at Zain and GTV as competitors, they would probably have laughed in your face. If you wrote an email to Amazon.com telling them that Books First, a little known Kenyan restaurant selling a few books on the side, would become a threat to their East African market, your email address would most likely be blacklisted.

The flat world also means brands will need to think global and local, hence the recently coined term, "glocal". To survive, brands have to be globally competitive and locally relevant. The entire globe is every brand's market now and originating from Japan, for example, does not mean Japan is your dominant market. Lexus, the luxury version of the ubiquitous Toyota, sells more cars in the United States than in Japan.

The Kenyan sugar industry, which for years has proved uncompetitive, may have to think twice as to whether all the local clamour and adulation of its nascent brands will be a match for global competition. The same applies to the brands in our tea, coffee and the infant business process outsourcing industry where proximity is even less of an issue.

The "long tail" and "flat world" phenomena portend an exciting future for brands. Human beings shall continue to need a few beacons to navigate choice. We shall therefore have a few really huge brands that promise consumers this seemingly contradictory combination of simplicity of access and complexity of choice. This will mean a consolidation of several brands into a few "big small brands". The primary purchase driver and brand building efforts shall shift from the huge variety of brands on offer to the "big small brand". This will not mean that the growth of small brands shall be checked; a bigger percentage will choke and die. Increased brand mortality rates in the era of the long tail will, however, not affect the length of the tail and variety shall continue to inundate us. The good news is the "big small brand" shall have stepped in to save us from ourselves by simplifying choice.

The world of brands is heading toward the era of the "big small brand", the brand that offers unlimited "long tail" variety of small (and big) brands to the consumer in one place. The one place could be online, at a physical location dotted conveniently around the flat world or even your mobile phone!

© Tom Sitati, 23rd August 2008.

The making of brand Germany

From soccer, sleek car brands, designer wear to body care products, Germany has top quality brands represented in virtually every category. So, does product brand make a nation brand or nation brand make the product brands? What can Kenya and our local brands learn?

As World Cups go, Germany is only beaten to the plate in terms of the number of World Cups won by magical Brazil and the tenacious Italy. If football prowess was all it took to be a world power then Brazil would rule the world. As a self-professed supporter of all things German, I am thankful that it is not football that determines nation brand rankings. The nation branding methodology pioneered by brand guru Simon Anholt places Germany in pole position.

The Anholt National Brand Index, which began in 2005, examines six key areas that affect "the way the world views the world". These include a country's exports, governance, tourism, culture and heritage, people, investment and immigration. The recently revamped study is now called The Anholt-GfK Roper Nation Brands Index. Simon Anholt now collaborates with public affairs research experts, Gfk Group. The latest results have an expanded list of 50 countries from the previous 35, with data being gathered from an even wider net of countries. But what makes brand Germany such a formidable force?

Culture of quality and discipline

The Mercedes Benz is undoubtedly Germany's chief ambassador. The prestigious line of motor vehicles boasts a reputation for superior engineering that has stood the test of time. This reputation can be traced back to the German companies' highly disciplined approach to creating and introducing brands to the market. This ensures the development of formidable brands that few nations are able to duplicate as superior quality is put first in every aspect. According to *Executiveplanet.com*, "A German manager believes deeply that a good quality production line and a good quality product will do more for the bottom line than anything else." This single-minded approach to building brands puts German brands in a class of their own. For this reason, German brands never compete on price – they do not need to.

Germany's healthy number of top brands camouflages what is really happening underneath. While the few giants almost appear inflexible, it is this consistency that keeps them winning. Professor Jeffrey Fear of Harvard Business School, when interviewed in 2005, highlighted the fact that beneath the larger global German brands are "thousands of owner-entrepreneur controlled *Mittelstand* (small and medium-sized firms) that remain very entrepreneurial, though in a quiet fashion.

Germany remains an export leader today because of those secretive firms."

This debate may never see a conclusion. The debate on whether a product brand makes a nation brand or nation brand makes the product brands ranks up there with the chicken and egg debate. For the sake of this short discussion, we shall assume that it doesn't matter whether the chicken came before the egg or the other way round. From Mercedes, BMW, Audi and Porsche in automobiles, SAP in business software, Nivea body care products, Boss cloth label to Adidas sportswear, Germany has top quality brands represented in virtually every category. As ambassadors for the German nation brand, they all reinforce Germany's quality reputation. The eggs in this case do transfer some credit to the chicken they came from as the eggs draw some credit from the chicken.

Deutschland mannshaft

It would be unfair to talk about Germany without talking about one of its greatest ambassadors – football. The World Cup is, in my opinion, one of the greatest global events. The jury is still out as to whether the Olympics might take that trophy but if I was the sole judge, I would give the trophy to the World Cup without bating an eyelid. This is my argument: one, the event grips the entire world regardless of economic level for the entire tournament and, two, most football fans will support a team at local, national and global level, ensuring global enthusiasm throughout the month-long tournament. Germany has stamped its national brand on this great global marketing event through its disciplined, almost precisely engineering approach to football exhibited by its team, Deutschland Mannshaft – literally translated as the "the machine" – this reputation has ensured a global following. A brand, after all, is nothing if it does not stand for something.

African nations can learn plenty from Germany. The country has been the aggressor in two world wars, gone through one of

the most shameful genocides in history and is the home of the
most infamous man – Adolf Hitler. No African nation brand
carries such a burden. Even South Africa with its apartheid
history, Zimbabwe with Mugabe, Somali's unending
statelessness, Rwanda's 1994 genocide, Nigeria's dodgy
reputation and Congo's unending conflicts are all pale compared
to Germany's history. If Germany can unearth what makes it
special among nation brands and excel at it through every point
of interaction with the globe, Africa still has great potential to
build some of the greatest nation brands on this planet.

*This article was published in the Business Daily on 18th
December, 2008.*

It's all about the brand

Branding is not a choice. If one does not intentionally brand, he or she will get branded anyway.

Personal branding, despite its seemingly obvious name, may not be that personal after all. A lot has changed since Tom Peters coined the term in 1997 in an article published in *Fast Company* entitled "Brand You".

Personal branding is about finding and leveraging unique, relevant attributes to further one's career. It borrows from the world of commercial branding. When successful, branding translates both into creating value for the brand owner in terms of profitability while also making the brand in question more valuable. To put it another way, successful branding ensures that the brand is both valued by customers (read employers or clients) while becoming valuable to the brand owner. The branding concept has its fair share of critics due to its focus on the long-term, sometimes at the expense of paying the bills. Yes, paying the bills today is critical as it guarantees that the brand owner shall be there to reap from that golden pot at the end of the brand rainbow.

Against African culture

Most African cultures place the community above the individual. One could, of course, argue that this is the culture that has more chiefs and kings than most. To counter this, one could argue that kings and chiefs were never personal brands but more of the embodiment of authority and even sometimes, like in the case of Egypt, deities. It was not personal; it was about creating an impersonal centre that could order society.

In the narrowest sense of the word, a brand is simply a name. For persons, the name is often the first distinguishing tool. In Africa, even the naming process betrays the underlying desire of society – to fail to distinguish. Children are named after their forebears who were in turn named after their forebears. In communities where this is practised strictly, what happens in effect is that most "personal brands" are not really personal. Virtually everyone is a "photocopy" of this or that ancestor. The naming part of branding is not really personal in this case; it is about the business of ordering society.

The media of one

The internet changed the world. The emergence of the interactive internet, termed Web 2.0, characterised by, among other innovations, social media absolutely changed the world of relationships. This applied to both personal and professional relationships. Relationships are at the heart of human interaction and branding too. Commercial brands, especially media brands, are reeling from the effects of new media. Personal branding has not been spared the effects either.

Platforms such as Facebook, MySpace and Twitter, which are now easily accessible via the mobile phone, have turned the world around its head. While one had to rely on mainstream media to communicate and thus grew their brand, now every individual with an internet connection is a media house. As a professional, you really do not need to address the whole world to move your career along. To get back to my point, even news now needs to be so focused that the best source is a relevant circle of individuals you can choose on Linked In or Xing.

Personal brands, like commercial brands, have a target audience determined by who will be most relevant in achieving your goals. Can we really get more focused than a chosen circle to interact with? To succeed in building one's personal brand using new media, one must remember that it is not personal, it is business.

Personal branding is not a choice

The centre has moved from the masses to the individual and personal branding has never been more important. An interesting thing about branding – and this applies to personal branding too – is that branding is not a choice. If one does not intentionally brand, they will get branded anyway by virtue of the attributes that keep emerging from their actions, image, interactions, the company they keep, the messages they send and to whom they choose to send these messages or vibes among all other points of interaction, both direct and indirect.

Even as things have changed, personal branding still remains what Tom Peters wrote about 12 years ago. It is about intentionally taking charge of what one stands for and leveraging it for career development. It starts with finding that core, then both embodying it and communicating it continuously and consistently so as to achieve the desired results in both the short and, more importantly, the long-term.

In the final analysis though, as things change, they really remain the same at the core. One major advantage the personal brand has over the commercial brand is that, even with society's manoeuvrings and all efforts towards conformity, there is, and can only be, one real you.

This article was published in the Business Daily on 30th June 2009.

Psst... shout by whispering

In a world full of shouting brands, go slow and let your brand interact with consumers rather than interrupt their lives.

Brands! Brands! Brands! Brand communication has become almost as ubiquitous as the sky above us. Billboards have replaced entire building facades, one can hardly watch a television programme without being interrupted by an advert or having a brand or two mentioned in the programme, and a radio session can hardly last 15 minutes without the mention of a brand. Even personal cell phones are no longer sacred. It is against this background that I feel brands may have gone too far and some drastic action is overdue.

I still maintain that brands are inevitable as they are the compasses we use to navigate choice. Brands are still the beacons we use to find our way around the world. This is the world that may have finally overdosed on offering options to a point where many consumers are now saying that enough is too much. The problem is not brands or branding per se, the problem is how brands have chosen to relate with us. The problem is that brand communication may have moved from satisfying our right to choice and creating relationships with us, to being rude interruptions to our already information loaded lives. How brands relate to us, and not brands in themselves, is what may require a rethink.

Malcolm Gladwell's famous book, "The Tipping Point," is full of groundbreaking ideas of how small things can have major long-term and far-reaching effects. The tipping point is defined as that specific place where the unexpected becomes the expected and a whole new trend, which the author terms an epidemic, is sparked off. In the first chapter, the business and science writer narrates how Hush Puppies, a brand that was virtually on its deathbed around 1994, increased its sales from 30,000 pairs of shoes to more than a million pairs and, in the same breath, set a fashion trend in the United States. The Hush Puppies Epidemic was set off by a couple of children from a not so fashionable neighbourhood who wished to be different. The rebirth of the Hush Puppies brand was sparked off in a very non-traditional, inexpensive and unobtrusive manner, aspects of which more brands would do well to borrow a leaf from.

New media such as the internet and mobile telephony offer brands an ideal platform to relate to consumers. More consumers now have the internet as part of their lives. Facebook, YouTube, Skype and other social networking media have become part and parcel of many consumers' lives. They do not see these platforms as an interruption but a welcome part of their lives; they see them as platforms that add value to their lives and conform to their lifestyles.

In his book "BrandDigital," the managing director of Landor Allen Adamson states: "It is important to identify where people are hanging out and what they are doing." This allows brands to "hang out" with consumers rather than become an interruption of what they already enjoy. Virgin Atlantic has a vibrant page on Facebook that has more than 8,500 fans. The social network, rather than interrupt what its consumers enjoy, has grown to become part of the consumers' lives and in the process allows existing and potential customers a comfortable forum to interact with the brand. Another great thing about it is that it does not cost much. Air France-KLM has Bluenity as its social network targeted at frequent fliers while Lufthansa has GenFly lounge targeting the student community. African brands continue to underestimate the power of new media much to their own detriment. Internet penetration in Africa may not be particularly impressive but the quality and influence of the population that is online commands a good fraction of the purchasing power of the continent.

The internet is now in an era christened Web 2.0, its hallmark being the collaborative nature of content creation. This means brands create portals to interact with consumers rather than communicate their brand messages in the one-sided manner we are traditionally used to. The Orange brand globally is aware of the power of Web 2.0 and thus have portals built around a lifestyle rather than the telephone. This makes the brand a welcome part of consumers' lives even as the brand benefits from a constant free flow of feedback.

In a room where everybody is shouting, your best bet of getting noticed is to shout louder than the loudest person. This strategy may work on the short-term because, ideally, that is what everybody in the room is trying to do. Brands find themselves in a marketplace that has become this room I refer to. It may be worth trying something radical – interact with rather than interrupt consumers' lifestyle. To do this, your brand does not need to be the loudest in the room; it just needs to shout by whispering.

This article was published in Business Daily on 17th February, 2009.

New media, new challenges and opportunities

As we enter the next phase of the internet, we are likely to see it impact our lives in even more profound ways.

What does branding have to do with new media? In my opinion, everything. Over time, brands have woven their way into our lives and they have done this to a fair degree by maximising on the power of various media channels. Any significant change in media introduces a material change in how brands are built, managed and experienced.

According to Microsoft's *Europe Logs on* study, "Europeans spent on average 8.9 hours per week, or 1.5 days a month, using the web in 2008, up 27 per cent from 2004." By 2010, Europeans will spend over 2.5 days a month on the internet. These numbers take on special significance when compared to the dwindling amount of time spent by the same population reading print media.

Print media in Kenya commands around 21 per cent of advertising revenue, according to media research firm Synovate's 2008 figures. This is about half of radio and slightly less than television.

Other parts of the world have recognised the slowed demand, and increasingly started to integrate media with the digital world, the space where readers influence content. In the US, print publications like the *Christian Science Monitor* have moved entirely online and in Europe, more than 75 per cent of newspapers allow readers to comment on articles. Recently, this figure has doubled in a short period of time, prompting Universal McCann to cite "consumer power as the biggest trend in marketing communications today." With over 65 per cent of online time being spent on communication, including email and social networks, this comes as no surprise.

Statistics such as these make it clear that the environment in which brands operate is changing rapidly everywhere in the world. The traditional path along which brand communication has been fashioned for decades has, until now, been linear and controlled by brands. This model appears to be on its way out, courtesy of the consumers' newfound power. With the advent of the internet connected world, the ground has shifted right underneath the feet of brands – and many have not even realised this yet. This presents both challenges and opportunities.

Force in the African market

No doubt, the internet is responsible for the growth of new media. According to *Europe Logs on*, Microsoft's April 2009 study on internet trends in Europe, the internet will overtake television as the medium of choice by June 2010. The findings have major implications for brands in terms of what consumer needs they satisfy, how they are positioned, communicated distributed, and even consumed.

As at December 2008, Africa had 54,171,500 internet users, representing a 5.6 per cent penetration rate. This is by no means impressive when you consider that North America has a 74.4 per cent internet penetration. And yet, while this may not change overnight, the fibre optic cable that went live in Kenya

(East Africa) in June 2009, is bound to cause major ripples.
Faster internet speeds combined with farther reach will make
the prophesied move from television to internet a reality.
Brands will find themselves increasingly unable to ignore this
development. Over the past five years, broadband connection in
Europe has grown by about 95 per cent! If a quarter of those
connections were in Kenya, it would totally change the media
consumption habits and alter the brandscape significantly.

According to statistics from the International
Telecommunication Union (ITU), Kenya's internet penetration
grew tenfold over eight years – from 0.7 per cent in 2000 to 7.9
per cent in 2008. This compares well with Africa's largest
economy, South Africa, which has an internet penetration of 9.4
per cent while Nigeria stands at 6.8 per cent. If one considers
that the cheaper, more accessible, real broadband internet will
soon be accessible via the mobile phone, the numbers are likely
to increase in the second half of 2009. It is not unrealistic to
assume that it may eventually hit the same stratospheric North
American (74 per cent) and European (48 per cent) levels.

Audiences glued to the screen, but which screen?

As internet penetration spikes, the number of eyeballs on the
computer screen will actually decline. According to *Europe Logs
On*, internet use of personal computers will drop to only about 50
per cent within the next five years. This, coming from the
present 95 per cent, is a huge shift. Eyeballs are set to move to
other gadgets such as IPTV, game consoles and mobile phones.

Kenya has nearly half its population (43.64 per cent according
to the Communications Commission of Kenya) now connected
via mobile phones. More than half the market that can be
counted upon to exercise what the economists call "effective
demand." This means that a majority of the mobile phone
consumers are actually in a position to desire to purchase
brands, and have the money (to varying degrees, of course), to
go ahead and make the purchase. The shift from computers to

cell phones is something for brands to follow keenly, especially as the content on mobile phones becomes more internet-driven. This is particularly true among youth and the so-called young at heart for whom the short message or phone call seem to be receding into history. As technology continues to evolve, it is important for brands to know which screen consumers are glued to.

New audience for brands

Wambui is the typical urban Kenyan teenager, straight out of high school and eager to explore the new world. She owns a mobile phone where she is able to keep in touch with her former schoolmates and the new buddies she meets virtually every day. Her new freedom allows her to go on unsupervised trips with her friends and hit the night spots that she could only dream off while ploughing through books in the strict boarding school environment she had been confined to for the past four years. Wambui's communication platform of choice is Facebook that allows her to share her thoughts, chat, send instant messages and even organise social events. Thanks to Orange, Safaricom, Yu and Zain – Kenya's mobile phone providers – she does not need to go to a cybercafé to log on to Facebook. She gets her news, hears about new trends and events, has her debates on issues both critical and trivial, is updated about Lindsay Lohan's love life, and can review Liverpool's match from her phone. Wambui even has a Liverpool fan club where she and fellow fans can discuss "their team".

Tumaini relocated to Boston in the US with his family 15 years ago when his British father and Kenyan mother decided to consolidate their US business interests. At 19, he is at the vanguard of the internet-led generation, which received a huge boost with the growth of broadband internet availability. Research by Netpop survey on internet usage in the US revealed that "over half who recently become aware of a new company, brand or product say they first learned about it from an online source." When the same respondents were asked what influenced them most into a purchase decision, family and

friends came first at about 60 per cent, followed by instant
messaging and chat rooms at 55 per cent. Considering that
Tumaini keeps in touch with family and friends spread across
three continents via social networking site Hi5, his brand
conversations are held online. The influence of family and
friends on his brand purchase decisions really comes to bear
online as well.

Both Wambui and Tumaini – and young customers like them –
suggest the shift from linear brand communication to networked
brand conversations. They signify the shift from producers in
one sphere and consumers on the other, to a network of players
who all cooperate to both create and consume brands. This has
created a totally new brandscape and it continues to evolve
daily. In order to stay relevant, brands must know where
internet-savvy customers like Wambui and Tumaini are
spending their time so they can be there. They need to know
what conversations they are having so they can make a
contribution to the discussion.

Web 2.0 and new consumer interaction

While the internet as we know it is about only two decades old, it
has matched and surpassed the changes that other sectors took
centuries to achieve within a fraction of that time. What began
as a few interconnected computers to share military data has
grown to become a vast network that includes mail systems,
media, academic institutions and large corporations.

As we enter the next phase of the internet – which has already
been dubbed Web 2.0 – we are likely to see the internet impact
our lives in even more profound ways. Whereas in the first phase
of the internet a few large brands acted as sources that
controlled information and commanded a huge audience, this is
increasingly being reversed. Web logs, social networking sites
such as Facebook, user-generated content sites like Wikipedia
and MySpace, chat rooms and mobile technology's dalliance with

the internet portend a radical shift, in which the audience plays almost as large, if not a larger role, than the big brands.

Web 2.0 has created a consumer that is not content on just listening. And this behaviour is not just limited to internet usage, but is now influencing how consumers interact with brands of every kind.

Web 2.0 and Henry Ford's Model T

"Any customer can have a car painted any colour that he wants so long as it is black." These are the famous words of Henry Ford. Around 1918, almost half the cars in the United Stated were Ford's famous Model T – and they were all black. This may have easily been a historical exaggeration but the point here is that Ford and many other industrialists to this day adopted a model that favoured the creation of a "one size fits all" mass-produced template that remained unchanged for years.

The Web 2.0 era has introduced a radical development where brands remain in beta (testing) phase for long periods of time. Some even go to the extent of being in perpetual beta, as users are always ready and thirsty for one more development (to which they will gladly contribute). What will it mean for brands if users demand the same from their cars, financial services, alcoholic beverages, confectionary and other brands they consume every day? Is it possible to, for example, to have a car that is continuously in beta mode such that one would theoretically occasionally take it back to the dealership for an "upgrade" or "software patch"?

Cooperate, don't control

What will it mean for your brand if consumers begin to demand more say in how your brand is created? What will it mean if the consumer finally lives up to what many academics have forecasted, and wants to tell you, the brand custodian, how best they wish to have their brand positioned?

Many of the Web 2.0 applications are built through the cooperation of a network of users. Some are specialists but most are average users, like you and me. The leading brands in this sphere are those that have found the best way to cooperate with users, taking their suggestions, and creating platforms that offer them a presence.

The long tail

Chris Anderson's publication, *The Long Tail*, is all about the tremendous potential in the 80 per cent we have tended to ignore on a day-to-day basis, due to our obsession with the few "hits". According to Anderson, this happens for music, movies, sports, professional life, and most definitely with brands.

In the Web 2.0 era, small websites, when combined, make up the bulk of the internet's content and, therefore, traffic. At the same time, the music that did not hit the Billboard charts, when combined, sells more than the music that hit the top ten. Anderson suggests that there is an opportunity to create a number of niche brands that dominate the 80 per cent the "hit brand" is bound to ignore. He also suggests that new media may be the platform where brands we are yet to even image will sprout and grow to prominence.

But if this is the reality, where will that leave brands that are still thinking about the 30-second television commercial and traditional mass marketing? Most likely, in the dustbin of history, unless they continue to evolve with the digital landscape. Brands succeed or fail depending on the extent to which they are able to profit from delighting consumer needs, wants, and even dreams – and, with consumers needs, wants and dreams in constant motion, brands will need to keep up in order to prosper.

This is no small task. Even as brands grapple with this "potential" future of the internet and Web 2.0, many are forecasting that Web 3.0 is already here. Nora Spivack, the founder of Radar Networks, is quoted in the Times Online as stating, "...we're now about to enter the third decade – Web 3.0 – which is about making the web much smarter." At this rate, we could be in Web 4.0 by the time you are done reading this paper!

Still, despite the fast pace, there are brands keeping up. Look to brands like Nike, which keeps its own social networking going, on its own platform. Users can share data, "compete" across borders, and celebrate together when they reach new milestones. There is also a Nike + blog that aggregates information from the larger community and creates a space for sharing and commenting on topics of interest to the community.

Look also to brands like Target, which has created a smart phone application that generates gift ideas. Brands like this are staying ahead of trends by embracing new interaction channels like blogs, social networking, and smart phones. These leading brands are working hard to evolve with their customers and are likely to be the leaders of the future as well.

This paper was first published on the Interbrand global website – www.interbrand.com in September 2009.

www.ingramcontent.com/pod-product-compliance
Lightning Source LLC
Chambersburg PA
CBHW020654160726
47991CB00003B/1182